THE CATHEDRAL
of Our Lady of the Angels

A House of Prayer for All Peoples

•

Mary Christine Foster

LOS ANGELES, CALIFORNIA

WELCOME

"A House of Prayer for All Peoples"

Whether you are one of over four million Roman Catholics in the Archdiocese of Los Angeles from Santa Barbara, San Fernando, San Gabriel, Los Angeles or San Pedro, or a pilgrim from Chicago, New York, London, Moscow, Shanghai, Seoul, Bethlehem, Doha, Cairo, Sydney or Santiago, the Cathedral of Our Lady of the Angels welcomes you.

Whether you are Catholic, Protestant, Jewish, Muslim, Buddhist, Hindu or not a member of a religion, the Cathedral of Our Lady of the Angels welcomes you.

Whatever age, race, nationality or color, welcome. Whatever language you speak, welcome.

You are the community for which the Cathedral was envisioned by Cardinal Roger Mahony and lead donor "angels" and built by thousands of human hands.

You are the people who inspired this magnificent house of worship, this place of inspiration and respite from the world's clamor.

Mary, the Mother of God, welcomes you to enter into the light of her Cathedral, to linger, to reflect on the mystery of her Son's death and Resurrection. She bids you to be nourished by His word and by His meal at the Eucharistic celebrations.

Mary welcomes you to her house to be inspired to love one another, to seek peace and justice for all her Son's people, to reach out to those less fortunate and share with them the bounty of God's loving care.

We welcome you with joy and love to your Cathedral, "a house of prayer for all peoples."

Rev. Monsignor Kevin Kostelnik
Pastor, Cathedral of Our Lady of the Angels

TABLE OF CONTENTS

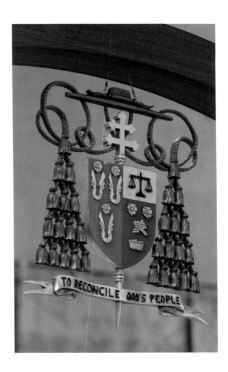

"Just as in heaven the myriad angels in their various orders all come together under the Queenship of one Woman, Mary, so in the 'City of Angels' the myriad peoples with the wonderful variety of their cultures and traditions all come together in the one Body of Christ and gather to praise God in the Mother Church of the Archdiocese of Los Angeles, the Cathedral of Our Lady of the Angels. May this Cathedral always remain an eloquent symbol of communion and fraternity, of mutual respect and understanding; may it be an enduring monument to Christian faith, hope and love, to Christian holiness!" - Pope John Paul II, August 5, 2002

*W*HERE ARE WE?

The Cathedral of Our Lady of the Angels is an important landmark and an integral part of the renaissance of downtown Los Angeles. Situated prominently on 5.6 acres of old Bunker Hill between Grand Avenue, Temple and Hill Streets and the Hollywood Freeway (101), the Cathedral unites the cultural and civic corridors of the city. The freeway flows along El Camino Real, the route blazed by Spanish missionaries as they carried the Gospel message in the 18th century. Within walking distance are the Music Center, Disney Concert Hall, the Museum of Contemporary Art, the Central Library, City Hall, the County Hall of Administration, Union Station and El Pueblo de Los Angeles.

A Cathedral overlooking a freeway?

When presented with the building site alongside the busy Hollywood Freeway 35 feet below, architect José Rafael Moneo was not perturbed. Just as many European cathedrals are built near rivers, such as Paris' Notre Dame on the Seine, he considered the freeway as Los Angeles' river of transportation, the connection of people to each other.

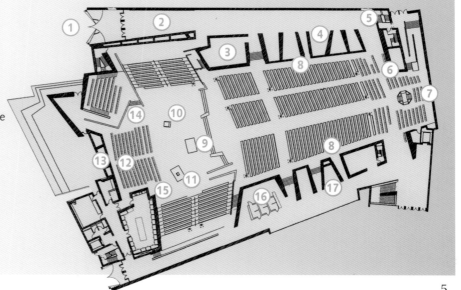

By July 30, 1999, the Cathedral's footprint was becoming visible at the corner of Grand (right) and Hill Streets, along the Hollywood Freeway.

Interior diagram of Cathedral

1. Bronze Doors
2. South Ambulatory
3. Blessed Sacrament Chapel
4. Our Lady of the Angels Chapel
5. Retablo
6. First of 12 Dedication Angels
7. Baptistry & Baptistry Tapestries, Ambry & Holy Oils, Paschal Candle
8. Communion of Saints Tapestries
9. Altar
10. Ambo
11. Cathedra
12. Presbyterium, Altar Tapestries
13. Architectural Cross
14. South Transept: Organ and Choir
15. North Transept
16. Reconciliation Chapel
17. Our Lady of Guadalupe Chapel

HISTORY OF THE DIOCESE

How did it begin?

Catholicism in California dates from the explorations of Spaniards Juan Rodriguez Cabrillo in 1542 and Sebastian Vizcaíno in 1602. These representatives of a Catholic power were accompanied by priests who first celebrated Mass on California shores.

CATHOLIC CHURCH IN CALIFORNIA MURAL

Frank Alonzo Martinez's mural in the south ambulatory depicts the Catholic Church's introduction into Alta California. It illustrates the Spanish expeditions, including the establishment of the first mission, San Diego de Alcala, in 1769. Native peoples are shown building and harvesting, as Mexican immigrants arrive to enrich the Church. Four additional murals will be added to bring California's Catholic history into the 21st century, leaving wall space for future generations to add their contributions.

Mural by
Frank Alonzo Martinez

The Catholic presence in the area now comprising the City of Los Angeles began on August 2, 1769, when Fray Juan Crespi named the "beautiful river from the northeast" *Nuestra Señora de Los Angeles de la Porciúncula*. Founded on September 4, 1781, by forty-four Hispanics from the San Gabriel Mission area, the tiny town was named after the river, *El Pueblo de Nuestra Señora de Los Angeles*.

Fray Junipero Serra, the *Presidente* of the California Missions, first walked the dusty pathways of the pueblo in 1782. Most inhabitants worshiped at the Old Plaza Church, where thousands of baptisms were recorded before the 1830s.

The First California Dioceses

In 1840 Pope Gregory XVI appointed Franciscan friar Francisco Garcia Diego y Moreno as the first bishop of both Californias (later specified as "Monterey"). Bishop Joseph Sadoc Alemany, a Dominican, transferred to San Francisco when it became a diocese in 1853. Then Monterey's Vincentian Bishop Thaddeus Amat

Over the Temple Street entrance to the plaza hangs a carillon that recalls California's early missions.

The Old Plaza Church ●

● Fray Junipero Serra

● Los Angeles in 1853

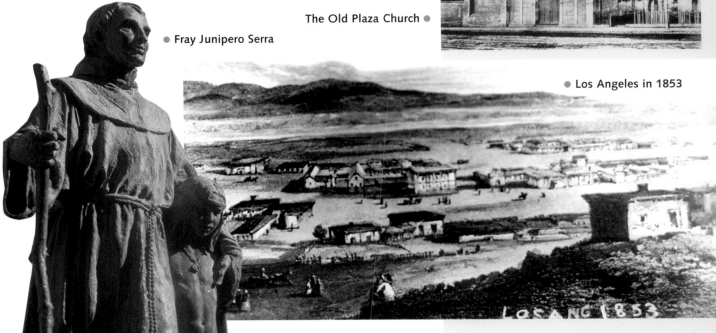

LOS ANG 1853

Cardinal James Francis McIntyre

moved the episcopal center to Los Angeles in 1859. Here he built the southland's first cathedral, St. Vibiana, between 1874 and 1876.

Los Angeles became a separate diocese in 1922 and an archdiocese in 1936. Its first archbishop, John J. Cantwell, established over fifty parishes. His successor, Cardinal James Francis McIntyre, built eighty-two parishes and increased Catholic schools from 141 to 347, about one a month for fifteen years.

Waves of immigration brought Chinese, Japanese, Vietnamese, Koreans and many other groups from Asia. The Hispanic population rose again. African Americans arrived in greater numbers from the American South. In 1970 Cardinal Timothy Manning addressed enormous ethnic and cultural changes, designating auxiliary bishops for the three-county area.

Los Angeles in the New Millennium

In 1985 Archbishop Roger M. Mahony became the first native Angeleno to shepherd the largest archdiocese in the country, leading 290 parishes in Santa Barbara, Ventura and Los Angeles Counties.

In 1991 he was named Cardinal. The Archdiocese of Los Angeles continues to meet great challenges with the assistance of *Nuestra Señora de los Angeles*.

Cardinal Roger M. Mahony, Archbishop of Los Angeles

*Around 1212 St. Francis of Assisi was given a small chapel on a tiny piece of property, a small portion – 'porziuncola' in Italian. From a fresco depicting the Blessed Virgin Mary surrounded by angels, the chapel became known as **Saint Mary of the Angels at the Little Portion**. The name "Los Angeles" derives from this Franciscan shrine.*

● **The right panel of the shrine of Our Lady of Guadalupe depicts children of Los Angeles.**

Why was a new "Mother Church" built?

St. Vibiana Cathedral

As early as 1859 Bishop Amat began to plan for a cathedral in Los Angeles. Construction commenced in 1872 on Main and Second Streets and was completed four years and $80,000 later. Archbishop Alemany of San Francisco dedicated the cathedral to Saint Vibiana in 1876.

Though he would have preferred a new, larger cathedral for his growing diocese, Bishop Cantwell chose to modernize and expand St. Vibiana between 1922 and 1924.

**Bishop Thaddeus Amat built
St. Vibiana Cathedral in the 1870s.**

**Architect José Rafael Moneo displays
an early model of the cathedral.**

The Journey to the New Cathedral Site

In 1996, when the City of Los Angeles condemned the earthquake-ravaged St. Vibiana Cathedral, approximately four million Catholics were left without a cathedral. The archdiocese needed accommodations for nearly three thousand people for special liturgies and services.

Plans called for the old church to be torn down and a new cathedral to be built on its site. However, historical preservationists demanded that the old cathedral be saved and incorporated into the new one. Such a proposal was costly and impractical.

On September 14, 1996, the Cathedral Advisory Board met with design architect Professor José Rafael Moneo to consider six possible locations in downtown Los Angeles. The site chosen was then a parking lot owned by the County of Los Angeles, which agreed to sell the property to the archdiocese.

The New Cathedral

Cardinal Roger Mahony's announcement of the decision to relocate also proclaimed that the new Cathedral's title would be "Our Lady of the Angels."

The official ground-blessing ceremonies took place on September 21, 1997. Construction began in October 1998 with work on the parking garage. Excavation of the foundations for the Cathedral began in May 1999. On March 19, 2002, Cardinal Roger Mahony placed the foundation-stone plaque inscribed with the words "My house shall be called a house of prayer for all peoples." - Isaiah 56:7. The formal blessing and dedication of the completed Cathedral took place on September 2, 2002.

"Today we... dedicate to your lasting service this house of prayer, this temple of worship, this home in which we are nourished by your word and your sacraments." - Cathedral **Dedication,** September 2, 2002

At the Mass of Dedication, Cardinal Mahony anoints the altar, which represents Christ, and on which the central actions of the Mass will take place.

During the dedication liturgy, Lovers of the Holy Cross Sisters honor the altar with incense and dance.

THE ARCHITECT AND HIS VISION

Designing a Sacred Space for Los Angeles

Rather than duplicating traditional Romanesque, Gothic or Baroque European designs, the Cathedral is steeped in memories of centuries of church designs, yet is a wholly new and vibrant expression of the 21st-century peoples of Los Angeles.

The Architect's Vision

The Cathedral architect, commissioned in 1996, is Professor José Rafael Moneo of Madrid, Spain, world-renowned recipient of the Pritzker Architecture Prize. He envisioned the building as "one of those examples where 20th-century architecture touched the sense of the sacred... and connected the people with the idea of the transcendent."

*A fifty-foot concrete cross **"lantern"** adorns the front of the Cathedral. At night its glass-protected alabaster windows are illuminated and can be seen at a great distance.*

"The people who walked in darkness have seen a great light." - Isaiah 9:1

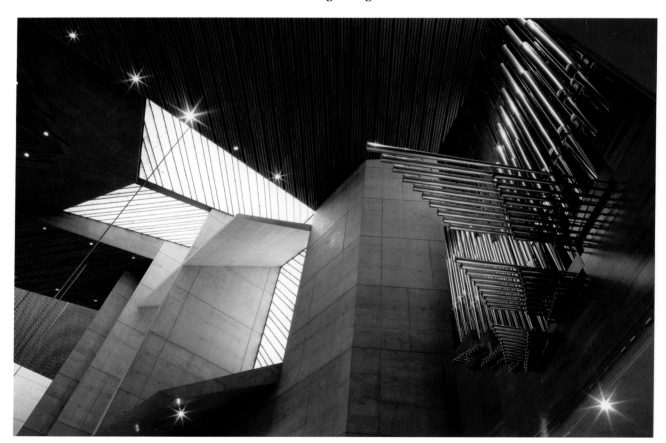

Capturing the sense of spiritual journey, the entrance to the Cathedral opens to a slightly inclined ambulatory that circles the interior and leads to the light of the nave. Away from, yet an integral part of a tumultuous Los Angeles, Moneo's towering Cathedral is a refuge, a spiritual sanctuary on our pilgrimage to the sacred.

**Architect Moneo
in the Communion procession
during the dedication liturgy.**

Two central theological truths guided Moneo's design. The first is that the Light of God is revealed in salvation history, especially in and through Jesus Christ. The second truth is the sense of journey that people make, alone and together, on the pilgrimage toward redemption in their lives and, ultimately, toward the fullness of the Kingdom of God in Heaven.

*"I am the light of the world.
Whoever follows me will not walk in darkness,
but will have the light of life." - John 8:12*

Inspired by these themes, the architect chose natural sunlight to flood the Cathedral through Spanish alabaster windows of milky white and earth tones. The asymmetrical walls reflect the intensity and hues of God's never-ending light in constant change, at one moment resplendent without shadows, at another moment subdued.

"The design's power stems from its aura of **timelessness**. *Few structures have been able to express the long arc of architectural history - from antiquity through classical Modernism - with such crystalline clarity."*

Nicolai Ouroussoff, L.A. Times critic

Cathedral Facts

Size of site:
5.6 acres

Size of Cathedral:
65,000 square feet

Height of Cathedral (interior):
55' above baptistry,
80' above altar,
95' above architectural cross,
135' above transepts

Seating in Cathedral:
2400 fixed, 600 moveable

Height of alabaster curtain wall:
Lowest point 20' above ground; highest 80'

Total area of alabaster windows:
27,000 square feet

Length of nave:
333'

"It's not about pizzazz and what
you see from the street.
It's all about **light** and space.
Those are the two essential
qualities of architecture."
Grant Mudford,
architectural photographer,
L.A. Times

"There is an abiding beauty
in the almost eternal silence
of these walls...
the serenity and **majesty**
bowl you over...."
Greg Goldin, architecture critic,
Los Angeles magazine

The Second Vatican Council
(1962-65) renewed Catholic
liturgy in ways that challenged
traditional church design
and inspired architects
to envision **communal** spaces
where the assembly
could surround the altar.

As in medieval churches,
the mass of the Cathedral
structure keeps it warm
in winter and cool in summer.
With visitors and lights
the **temperature** in the nave
remains about
70-74 degrees Fahrenheit.

The fact that Grand Avenue is
35 feet higher than Temple
Street partially inspired the
position of the Cathedral on
the **high ground** and its entry
facing the plaza.

BUILDERS OF THE CATHEDRAL

The Dream Becomes Reality

Many historic cathedrals took centuries to construct. The eleven-story-high Cathedral of Our Lady of the Angels was completed between May 1999 and the summer of 2002. This was the first Roman Catholic cathedral erected in the western United States in thirty years.

The building of the 65,000-square-foot Cathedral was a technological feat of the computer age. To achieve over 800 angles in the geometrically complex design, the layout superintendent plotted more than 11,000 points in three-dimensional space. Extensive testing and calculation indicated that the architectural concrete had to be poured in the dark of night to keep the water below 70 degrees and ensure 500 years of durability. None of the concrete forms could vary by more than 1/16th of an inch.

"The places where we worship **shape the way we pray**, and the way we pray shapes the way we live."
Rev. Richard S. Vosko, liturgical consultant

15

Construction employed state-of-the-art features to meet the special needs of our locale and to make the Cathedral a building for the ages. The 151-million-pound structure rests on 198 rubber isolator pads and sliders that are three feet thick. These enable it to float laterally as far as 27" during a magnitude 8.3 earthquake on the San Andreas Fault or an 8.0 on the downtown faults.

The nave walls form the back of the ambulatory chapels. The two sides are tied together at the top by a huge concrete girder. Structural steel trusses connect the sides and support the roof. The chapel walls extend down to the foundation. The Cathedral does not actually rest upon the ground, but upon the base isolators. Millions of pounds bear down directly, yet each isolator, sandwiched between steel plates, compresses only about 1/16th of an inch.

*"The Cathedral is a place where **all are welcomed,** where all may find rest from their labors, where all may be renewed in body and spirit, where all may be transformed and ... from where all may go forth to live and proclaim the Gospel." - Rev. Richard Vosko, liturgical consultant,* The Tidings, *August 30, 2002*

By March 1, 2001, the Cathedral was taking shape. In the foreground are the Cathedral Conference Center and parking facility (left) and Cardinal's residence (right).

On the roof of the conference center an intricate solar panel system generates between 10% and 15% of the total energy needed for the complex – part of the Church's commitment to environmental stewardship.

Copper roofing was selected for durability. Concealed gutters divert rainwater into the street. The geometry of the roof is highly articulated and ornamental, with the secondary steel framing off the flat main body and skylights invisible except from a great distance.

The wall dots show where steel rods held poured concrete forms together. When the forms were stripped away and the rods removed, holes were left and were filled with lead plugs to keep out water, insects, etc.

A Labor of Love

Clustered in the rafters nearly 100 feet above the altar are nine scripture verses on laminated plaques signed by the owners and workers of WoodCeilings, Inc., "in order to honor the Lord and acknowledge

Workers carefully lower the six-ton altar into the sanctuary before the roof is constructed over the space.

the privilege we have felt working on this project." Directly over the altar is the text "In my house, says the Lord, 'everyone who asks, receives; and the one who seeks, finds; and to the one who knocks, the door will be opened.' - Matthew 7:8"

*"This is **a job like no other**. It's something you feel. The work of the people in the field came through with their hands and into their work. Take a look at the craftsmanship. You see the translation of their hearts coming in through their hands."* - Audre Kleven, senior project manager, **Morley Builders**, The Tidings, Aug. 30, 2002

Over 2,000 designers, architects, and construction workers and builders worked over six years on the entire Cathedral complex. The union men and women who laid the limestone floor, framed the alabaster windows, poured the concrete, raised the roof, placed the wires and pipes, etc., speak of the spiritual influence this job had on themselves and their families.

*"The workers had an **esprit de corps** different from any other project. They didn't walk places – they ran to get things."* - Randy Fulton, project manager

Ed Lohr and (behind him) Louis Carnevale seal the relics of saints into the floor beneath the altar during the dedication liturgy. Their firm was responsible for the stone masonry on the Cathedral.

- *Design Architect: Professor José Rafael Moneo*
- *Executive Architect: Leo A. Daly Company*
- *General Contractor: Morley Construction Company*
- *Landscape Architect: Campbell & Campbell*
- *Structural Engineer: Nabih Youssef & Associates*
- *Liturgical and Public Art Consultant: Reverend Richard S. Vosko*

STATUE OF THE VIRGIN MARY

Our Lady of the Angels

Sculptor Robert Graham created the eight-foot bronze statue of Our Lady of the Angels for the ornamental space above the Cathedral doors. She is a woman for all ages, serene and strong, favored by God to be the mother of Jesus, an example of discipleship for all Christians.

The modern figure is presented as "a woman clothed with the sun, with the moon under her feet" (Revelation 12:1). She now shares the glory of the Risen Christ in the fullness of God's presence. The opening behind her head creates a halo shaft of God's light shining on her as the sun travels from east to west.

The Patroness of Los Angeles

This image of Mary uniquely suits her ethnically rich namesake city of Los Angeles. Her face blends Asian, African American, and Caucasian traits. The thick braid down her back suggests Native Americans and Hispanics. Her wide-sleeved dress is coolly suitable for Southern California.

*"She could be the **woman** piloting the No. 3 bus along Sunset Boulevard, the one who served you lunch today in Little Tokyo or wiped your brow as you lay in a Boyle Heights hospital bed. She could even be that statuesque supermodel type... breezing by on the Santa Monica Promenade."*
Reed Johnson, L.A. Times

•

*"**Mary**. Full of grace. The gift of God's own life pulses through the fabric of her being and is given to us through her."*
Dr. Michael Downey, theologian,
The Cathedral at the Heart of Los Angeles

•

"My soul proclaims the greatness of the Lord; my spirit rejoices in God my savior."
Luke 1:46, 47 (The **Magnificat**)

The Threshold

Church doors symbolize the entrance into sacred space on our journey of faith. Mexican-born Los Angeles sculptor Robert Graham designed the 25-ton, 30' x 30' bronze doors on the southeast side of the Cathedral. It includes a 10' tympanum over huge doors and smaller doors set within them.

The Outer Doors

The immense doors that frame the entryway, each in the shape of an inverted L, are hollow, narrowing from 30" thick at the far left and right to just 1" in the middle. They open easily, turning on steel posts with a sophisticated hydraulic system. On each door, diagonal lines form triangles, evoking the Holy Trinity and pointing upward to the statue of Mary.

●

"The Church Doors symbolize a bridge over which we may travel back and forth over ages and systems of belief."
- Robert Graham

The Inset Doors

On the smaller, inset doors, a grapevine in relief symbolizes the Church. Among its leaves are 40 ancient symbols representing pre-Christian images from Europe, Asia, Africa and North America.

Above these symbols are representations of fifteen Marian apparitions, from European origins, that have been filtered through the indigenous cultures of the New World.

Left: Above the Sorrowful Mother are implements of her Son's Crucifixion.

*"I am the **gate**. Whoever enters through me will be saved, and will come in and go out and find pasture."*
John 10:9

•

*"Ask and you will receive; seek and you will find; **knock** and the door will be opened to you."*
Luke 11:9

•

*Robert **Graham's** other large-scale sculptures include the 1984 L.A. Olympic Gateway, the Duke Ellington Memorial in Central Park, and the F.D.R. Memorial in Washington, D.C.*

Right: The All-Powerful Hand honors Jesus' mother, foster-father, and grandparents.

Diagram for Ancient Symbols

(Left door, beginning first row on left, top to bottom)

1. Goose
2. Southwest Indian Flying Serpent
3. Chumash Man

4. Peacock Barge
5. Griffin
6. Chinese Turtle

7. Ibis
8. Griffin
9. Fish
10. Hand of God
11. Eagle (St. John the Evangelist)
12. Dove
13. Bee

14. Celtic Serpents
15. Stag
16. Croatian Cross
17. Chumash Condor
18. Peacock
19. Falling Man
20. Tree of Jesse

(Right door, beginning first row, top to bottom)

21. Energy (soul)
22. Lion (St. Mark the Evangelist)
23. Water
24. Lamb
25. Hand (listening symbol)
26. Chinese/Japanese Heaven Symbol

27. Pair of Ostriches
28. Rooster
29. Bull (St. Luke the Evangelist)
30. Trefoil (Celtic Trinity)
31. Dog (loyalty)
32. Sicilian Legs (regeneration symbol)
33. Bull
34. Foot

35. I Ching / Tai Chi
36. Samoan Kava Bowl
37. Serpent/Dragon

38. Celtic Monster
39. Raven Eating Man's Liver
40. Dolphin

Diagram for Manifestations of the Virgin

(Left door, left to right)

1. **Virgin of Pomata** - This image from an Andean village comes from the late-colonial School of Cuzco. Mary wears a feathered Inca headdress and a billowing dress suggestive of Pachamama, the Inca mountain goddess.
2. **Apocalyptic Virgin/Immaculate Conception** - Inspired by Revelation 12, Mary is depicted with powerful wings crushing the satanic serpent. The lily symbolizes purity.
3. **Ex Voto to Virgin of Guadalupe** - A mother offered this picture at the Guadalupe shrine as an ex voto ("fulfilling a vow" - Latin), thanking Mary for intercession on behalf of her sick child.
4. **Divine Shepherdess** – the depiction of Mary

reclining in a field with four sheep commemorates her appearance to a Spanish monk.

5. **Virgin of the Candlestick with Virgins of Belén** - Mary is shown in a billowing dress (School of Cuzco). She holds a blanket and cradles the infant Jesus. Smaller images show her appearances in Belén, Peru.

6. **Virgin of the Rosary of Chichinquira** – Mary with St. Andrew (right) and St. Anthony (left). St. Anthony, "the Christographer," is depicted with Jesus on a book. Robert Graham used his mother's rosary for this image.

7. **Virgin of Mercy** – Mary's cloak protects souls in Purgatory (pictured, right).

(Right door, left to right)

8. **Virgin of Guadalupe** – Memorializing Mary's appearance to Aztec peasant St. Juan Diego, the image depicts the thornless roses she instructed him to pluck in December 1531. The moon and sun are from the Book of Revelation.

9. **Virgin of the Cave** - In the Spanish Caribbean this image, miraculously recovered from a cave, was associated with miracles.

10. **Virgin of Monserrat** - This image from Catalonia, Spain, is one of Europe's "Black Madonnas."

11. **Pietá** - A popular portrayal: Mary embraces her Son's body.

12. **Chalice with Sheep** - The sheep of Christ's flock drink His blood, which spurts from His pierced hand (the All-Powerful Hand) into the chalice of the Eucharist.

13. **Mater Dolorosa, the Sorrowful Mother** – Above Mary are the implements used in her Son's Crucifixion.

14. **La Mano Todopoderosa, the All-Powerful Hand** – With Jesus in the center, Saints Anna, Mary, Joseph and Joachim are depicted on the fingers. Anna and Joachim are names given to Mary's parents.

15. **Virgin of Loreto with Litany of Loreto** – Mary is depicted with angels and poetic titles from the Litany of Loreto. The addition of "Queen of Poland" honors the visit of Pope John Paul II to Los Angeles.

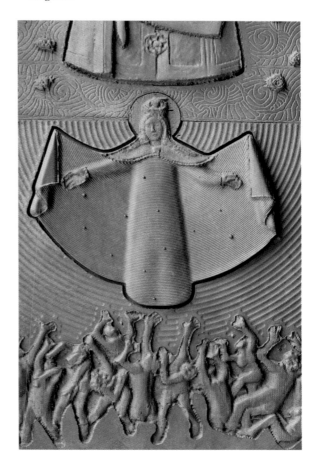

THE BAPTISTRY

The Water of Salvation

A t the plaza's Gateway Pool, we are promised "living water" to satisfy our spiritual thirst. On our spiritual journey our desire is fulfilled at the baptismal font. Baptism washes us clean from sin and incorporates us into the life of Christ and his Church.

"Let us approach with a sincere heart and in absolute trust, with our hearts sprinkled clean from an evil conscience and our bodies washed in pure water." - Hebrews 10:22

Designed by liturgical consultant Father Richard Vosko, the font accommodates Baptism by immersion for adults and infants. Its ancient octagonal form frames a cross. The eight sides reflect Christ's Resurrection on the "eighth day" (two days after his Crucifixion on Friday, the sixth day of the week).

Persons being baptized descend the steps in sinfulness and emerge transformed and renewed in Jesus Christ, into the nave where God's people welcome them to share the Eucharistic banquet.

The fish design in the baptismal font's gates recalls the Greek word IXCTHUS (fish), an acronym of Greek words meaning "Jesus Christ, Son of God and Savior." Early Christians used the fish as a secret symbol to identify themselves to one another during times of persecution for the faith.

The Baptism of Jesus

John Nava's tapestry for the baptistry shows Jesus being baptized by Saint John the Baptist. The humility of both is unforgettable.

*"After **Jesus** was baptized, he came up from the water and behold, the heavens were opened [for him], and he saw the Spirit of God descending like a dove [and] coming upon him. And a voice came from the heavens, saying, 'This is my beloved Son, with whom I am well pleased.'" - Matthew 3:16-17*

The Ambry

Jefferson Tortorelli designed the ambry, the cabinet for holy oils, from Australian jarrah wood with hand-cast glass doors from Judson Studios. It contains blown-glass vessels designed by Sacramento artist Marirose Jelicich. They hold holy oils blessed each year at the Holy Week Chrism Mass and sent to parish communities for use in the Church's sacramental life: anointing of catechumens, Baptism, Confirmation, Anointing of the Sick, and Ordination to the Priesthood.

The Paschal Candle

The candle-stand near the baptismal font holds the Paschal candle (placed near the altar during Easter time). Designed by Marirose Jelicich, it weighs over three hundred pounds and is fabricated with powdercoated aluminum with three satin-finished aluminum angels.

The newly baptized receive a candle lighted from the Paschal candle, shown here, as a reminder to radiate Christ's light to the world.

THE NAVE

Into the Light

The nave is seen here from the presbytery, looking toward the baptistry.

O n our spiritual journey to the altar, we enter into the light of the nave, where the faithful gather for the Eucharistic celebration. Fixed seating allows for 2400 people, and moveable seating can accommodate an additional 600, including 400 priests in the presbyterium area behind the altar.

Alabaster Windows

The Cathedral features the largest use of alabaster windows in the United States – some 27,000 square feet. The powerful natural light that they admit to this space is part of the beauty of creation and symbolizes God's grace.

*"For you were once darkness,
but now you are light in the Lord.
Live as children of light." - Ephesians 5:8*

•

*The lights in the nave surround trumpet-shaped cones containing the speakers for the sound system. The **acoustics** are superb.*

*Natural **alabaster** has an unusual translucency because it contains moisture and oil in addition to various mineral deposits. The vein patterns of red, gray, gold, brown and green found within alabaster were created millions of years ago when it was in the form of liquid rock mixing elements of dinosaurs, insects, plants and dirt.*

The nave and the two transepts are designed to encourage full, conscious and active participation of the entire congregation in the liturgy. No pillars block vision, because nine steel trusses and the chapel structures on each side support the soaring ceiling. The dynamic effect results from architect Moneo's design, that avoids right angles and symmetry.

In traditional style the Cathedral faces east, the direction of Jerusalem and the rising sun. Its cruciform structure represents the cross on which Jesus died.

The 60,000 stones paving the floor with Spanish Jana limestone emanate in a circular pattern from the altar, the Cathedral's spiritual center.

Spanish alabaster panels were cut from 5-6 foot boulders to the thickness of 3/4" and vary in size from 2 1/2' to 6' wide. Their careful positioning creates giant mosaics, covering the 60' x 100' north and south walls. Smaller panel windows are on the northeast and west sides of the building. Large slanted shafts of alabaster in the devotional chapels are reminiscent of the interior light shafts used by the early Franciscans when they designed the California Missions.

*Norberto Gutierrez manufactured the cherry wood **pews** and the movable chairs at The Wood & Iron Factory in Tijuana, Mexico.*

When alabaster reaches about 120 degrees Fahrenheit in test ovens, it decomposes into gypsum, becoming chalky and opaque. Therefore, an **exterior** layer of glass, covered with a chevron-patterned protective film to control ultraviolet rays and heat, shields the alabaster. Cool air circulates between the glass and alabaster layers. Exhaust fans draw out hot air.

The Architectural Cross

Above the altar is a large architectural cross. Light pours into the Cathedral along the slanted crossbeam. At night it shines a beacon of light to the outside. The cross is an emblem of Christ, "the Light of the World."

The architectural cross is over the altar.

*T*HE TAPESTRIES

The Communion of Saints

"Greet one another with a holy kiss. All the holy ones greet you." - 2 Corinthians 13:12

*"You are fellow citizens with the holy ones and members of the **household** of God, built upon the foundation of the apostles and prophets, with Christ Jesus himself as the capstone. Through him the whole structure is held together and grows into a temple sacred in the Lord." - Ephesians 2:19-21*

The tapestries created by California artist John Nava are the largest collection hanging in a Catholic church in the United States. Throughout the ages pictorial wall cycles have told vividly the stories of the Greek, Roman, Medieval and Renaissance periods. Nava's Communion of Saints is part of this heritage, yet unique to the 21st century.

The Communion of Saints on the south and north walls of the nave include 25 tapestries depicting 136 holy people, some formally acknowledged as "saint" and "blessed." They include the Apostles, saints and martyrs of the early Church, saints of all languages, nationalities and cultures, and those particular to the United States. They are females and males of all ages, races, occupations and vocations from around the world. Twelve anonymous figures, including children, represent the many anonymous holy people in our midst.

Nava blended digital imaging and "Old Master" methods. He constructed figures from multiple studies, combined drawn and painted elements,

Saints Elizabeth Ann Seton (2nd from left), Elizabeth of Portugal (2nd from right) and André Bessette are seen with an anonymous mother and child and two little girls.

had costumes made when needed, and even drafted family members as models. Nava's hope is for people to identify and see that "a saint could look like me."

To meet the deadlines involved and to replicate his images in the weaving, Nava developed a method of making digital files of the designs. The digital files were e-mailed from Nava's studio in Ojai, California, to Flanders Tapestries near Bruges, Belgium. Digitally programmed looms wove according to his designs. A project that scores of weavers working dozens of looms would have needed decades to produce in the 16th century, took twenty months of designing and two months of weaving in the 21st century.

All of the tapestries are made from cotton with a small percentage of viscose to assure that the colors endure – a subtle interplay of neutral tones evocative of ancient Italian frescoes. Cotton woven by the Egyptians has survived intact for thousands of years.

The large stone-texture patterns in the background are from actual scans of excavations of the Via Dolorosa in Jerusalem from Biblical times.

Pictured here are (from left) John Baptist de la Salle, Paul Chong Hasang, Moses the Ethiopian, Kateri Tekakwitha and Thomas More.

All the tapestry figures direct our eyes toward the Eucharistic celebration, centered upon the altar. This panel shows (from left) Bruno, Anselm and Bartholomew and Mother Teresa of Calcutta and John XXIII.

The procession toward the altar includes (from left) Bonaventure, Peter Claver, Andrew, Felicitas and Perpetua.

The Altar of Angels

The altar is the central and most important liturgical feature of the church. It represents Christ. Nourished by God's word and by the bread and wine of the Eucharist (from the Greek word meaning "thanksgiving"), the assembly gives thanks for God's salvation through Christ's death and resurrection.

The altar table is eight by ten feet, and ten inches thick.

Flanked by concelebrants, Cardinal Roger Mahony elevates the chalice during the Eucharistic celebration of the Cathedral's dedication. The cloths spread upon the altar come from around the world. Their arrangement mimics the pattern of the different woods in the back of the cathedra, from many parts of the world.

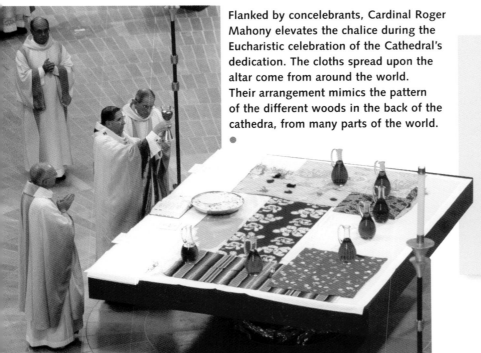

Twenty-six relics are sealed into the floor under the altar by a stone marked with a tiny red cross. Represented among them are Saints Patrick, Benedict, Gregory the Great, Francis of Assisi, Catherine of Siena, Rose of Lima, Martin de Porres, Elizabeth Ann Seton, John Neumann, and Charles Lwanga and Blessed Kateri Tekakwitha and Junipero Serra.

Cardinal Roger Mahony designed the altar in consultation with artisan Louis Carnevale. A six-ton slab of Turkish Rosso Laguna marble was fabricated, cut, and polished in Carrara, Italy. Because of its size, it had to be lowered into place by a crane before the roof was installed.

"Since the Church teaches that 'the altar is Christ,' its composition should reflect the nobility, beauty, strength, and simplicity of the One it represents." - National Council of Catholic Bishops, Built of Living Stones: Art, Architecture and Worship, #56

The marble is a rich burgundy color with veins of white, gray and red. The altar table rests upon a single round pillar of similar marble. It is the center of the pattern in the limestone floor. The grace and power of the Eucharist seem to flow throughout the Cathedral.

Altar Angels

Four delicately fashioned angels designed and sculpted in bronze by Los Angeles artist Mary Louise (M.L.) Snowden curve around the base of the altar. She was inspired by the passage

"Another angel came and stood at the altar, holding a gold censer. He was given a great quantity of incense to offer, along with the prayers of all the holy ones, on the gold altar that was before the throne." – Revelation 8:3

"Since the time of the ancient Greeks, mastering the curved relief is the most difficult of all sculpture challenges."
Remo Nevi, art critic

Altar Tapestries

Seven tapestries behind the altar depict a schematic map of downtown Los Angeles converging with the circular, 11th century "Cosmati" pattern traditionally associated with divinity. Woven into the tapestries are words from the Book of Revelation reflecting the union of God and humanity: *"See, God's dwelling is among mortals. God will dwell with them. They will be God's people and God will be with them."* - Revelation 21:3

All four angels together weigh close to one half ton and are sculpted around a stabilizing core of bronze with layers of silver and heavy pure gold bullion.

THE CATHEDRA AND AMBO

To Teach, To Govern and To Sanctify

The Cathedra

A cathedral is more than simply a large church. What distinguishes it is the bishop's cathedra (Latin for "chair"). From this ceremonial chair the Archbishop of Los Angeles exercises his leadership responsibilities of teaching, governing and sanctifying.

Jefferson Tortorelli designed a chair that fits human proportions but has a presence corresponding to the Cathedral's scale. It is made of woods from every continent except Antarctica. From the basic chair of Australian jarrah wood, two ebony arms extend as if welcoming the assembly.

Linked crosses on the back are made of ebony and curly pink ivory wood (Africa), amboyna burl (Thailand), olivewood (Israel), carob (Lebanon), lacewood (Europe), purple heart (Central/South America), cocobolo (Central America), vera wood (Venezuela), and holly (North America). They represent many diverse peoples, drawing strength from being linked together.

Tortorelli used the age-old techniques of joinery in constructing the 800-pound cathedra, instead of mechanical fasteners or glue.

Cardinal Roger Mahony's coat of arms symbolizes his mission as a bishop.

● The cathedra is the archbishop's ceremonial chair.

*"I have truly been blessed... I am able to **create** with my mind and hands pieces that will be used in the worship space of a community. I cannot think of a more rewarding endeavor." - Jefferson Tortorelli, liturgical artist*

At the Cathedral ambo, lector Jim Devlin proclaims the word of God.

Cathedral Galeros

Hanging from the ceiling directly over the cathedra area are two galeros, the red hats bestowed on cardinals for over a millennium. These galeros belonged to Los Angeles' previous Cardinal-Archbishops James Francis McIntyre and Timothy Manning.

The Ambo

At the ambo, the words of Sacred Scripture are proclaimed. The word *ambo* has a Greek origin, signifying a mountain or elevation.

Jefferson Tortorelli's design was inspired by an account in the Gospel of Matthew; Jesus walked to the top of a mountain, turned, and taught the people. There was no barrier between him and his listeners.

The ambo is constructed primarily of reddish toned, Australian jarrah wood. The exterior has accents of red blood wood, sometimes called cardinal wood or satine. Tortorelli used a special blend of oils to enhance the colors.

The adjustable table is accessible to all – a child, a person in a wheelchair, or a seven-foot-tall basketball player. Its steel internal mechanism is fully mechanical, not electric, so it can last centuries with minimal maintenance.

The Saving Grace of Jesus

S ince the Cathedral's dedication, hundreds of thousands of pilgrims have kissed or touched the feet of Simon Toparovsky's sculpture of Jesus crucified, burnishing the dark bronze patina to gold.

Toparovsky has depicted the brutality of crucifixion in the body's agony. Yet Jesus' serene facial expression shows his triumph over sin and death.

The six-foot human form was cast in one piece. The surface shows flayed and abraded skin. The figure is misshapen from swelling, the hands in spasm from the nails. The plant *euphorbia mili*, which grows in the Holy Land and is commonly called "crown of thorns," surrounds the head. Toparovsky used sycamore for the 14-foot cross, following an ancient legend about the wood used on Calvary.

THE CRUCIFIX

Toparovsky's sculpture represents Jesus moments before death, following the research into crucifixion detailed by French surgeon Pierre Barbet in his book *A Doctor on Calvary*.

Reverence paid to the crucifix during the Good Friday liturgy, 2004, expresses the congregation's response to Jesus, whose suffering and death it represents.

"It was impossible for me not to really feel the **suffering**," to understand "that I could embrace everything that was hard in my life... to be the most open channel for portraying Jesus that I could." - Simon Toparovsky, sculptor

•

"Then Pilate took Jesus and had him scourged. And the soldiers wove a crown out of thorns and placed it on his head...." - John 19: 1-2

•

"When Jesus had taken the wine, he said, **'It is finished.'** And bowing his head, he handed over the spirit." - John 19:30

DEDICATION ANGELS AND LITURGICAL VESSELS

Inspiring Worship Through Beauty

The Dedication Angels

Twelve bronze dedication candleholders designed and fabricated by sculptor Max DeMoss adorn the nave walls. Playful bronze and silver angels with outstretched wings – "beings of light," says the artist – adorn the candleholders.

Angels are mentioned at least 108 times in the Old Testament and 165 times in the New Testament. The Greek word aggelos *means "messenger."*

During the Cathedral's dedication, the Sign of the Cross was traced with holy oil on the wall under each candle. According to a cathedral tradition in the Catholic Church, the candles were lighted for the first time on the dedication day and will be lighted again on each anniversary.

Reverend Msgr. Terrance L. Fleming anoints the Cathedral wall in the north transept during the dedication.

Each whimsical angel has individual characteristics and gestures. DeMoss wants the "angels' gestures to be welcoming, to greet the viewer." As people enter the nave, they see one angel, then another and another, until there is an "Aha!" a sudden awareness that a host of angels accompanies them toward the altar.

"I saw an angel standing on the **sun.** *He cried out [in] a loud voice to all the birds flying high overhead, 'Come here. Gather for God's great feast.'" - Revelation 19:17*

The foot-tall chalices have removable, individually blown glass cups above hammered, solid aluminum stems, connected by nodes of the same Turkish Rosso Laguna marble used for the altar. The flagons (decanters) for the sacramental wine are blown glass surrounded by an angel motif. Sterling silver stoppers are decorated with Rosso Laguna marble. The shallow aluminum patens (plates) used for the bread are hammered-finished outside and satin-finished inside.

Liturgical Vessels

Sacred vessels hold a place of honor in the Eucharistic celebration, especially the chalice and paten, which are used in presenting, consecrating, and receiving the wine and bread. Artist Marirose Jelicich designed all liturgical vessels, processional sets and the Paschal-candle stand. Their simple elegance and timelessness reflect dignity and spiritual power.

On this side of the processional cross, the liturgical seasons are represented with the colors of red, green, white and purple.

The processional cross is eight feet tall, made of satin-finished aluminum. At the top, two aluminum angels hold a three-foot cross incorporating blown glass with semi-precious stones: yellow citrine, blue lapis lazuli, blue topaz and clusters of pearls set in sterling silver. Colors on one side represent the liturgical seasons. Blue and aqua on the reverse symbolize Our Lady of the Angels.

Aluminum stems, glass bowls, and marble nodes make up the chalices.

THE CHAPELS IN THE AMBULATORIES

For the Devotion of the Faithful

The Second Vatican Council called for the assembly of the faithful to share in one celebration of the Eucharist at a church's main altar. Therefore, the ten side chapels on the main floor open onto the ambulatories rather than onto the nave. These chapels are intended to foster devotional prayer and meditation. Most are intentionally left unfinished, awaiting devotional developments in future generations.

The Blessed Sacrament Chapel

The Blessed Sacrament Chapel in the south ambulatory is signaled by two bronze-and-silver candle sconces designed by Max De Moss. The wheat and grape motif, a key element of the tabernacle, is repeated in the sconces.

When the tabernacle is open, it forms a triptych. The sacred vessel containing the Blessed Sacrament is in the center.

The chapel is dedicated to the Blessed Sacrament, the Eucharist consecrated at Mass and reserved here, to be taken to the sick and homebound. Natural light filters through an alabaster shaft, complemented by the original chandeliers from the old St. Vibiana Cathedral.

The large bronze tabernacle, designed by De Moss, refers to the Jewish Ark of the Covenant. The Ark held the tablets of the Ten Commandments given to Moses, signifying the bond between God and God's people. Two angels, sculpted in adoration over the Ark, bore witness to God's enduring presence with the people.

The Cathedral's tabernacle gives the impression of a scroll, containing God's word. Sculpted sheaves of wheat, grape leaves and grape clusters represent bread and wine, consecrated as the Body and Blood of Christ in a new covenant.

When the cylindrical form is open, sentinel angels are visible. De Moss's bronze lamp burns continuously to remind us of Christ's presence in the Blessed Sacrament reserved in the tabernacle.

Our Lady of the Angels Chapel

A chapel along the south ambulatory honors Our Lady of the Angels. In the 1950s, Cardinal James Francis McIntyre commissioned the porcelain, 8-foot, Baroque statue of Our Lady of the Angels by artist Professor Eugenio Pattarino of Florence, Italy. The statue once stood in St. Vibiana Cathedral. It offers a cherished traditional depiction of Mary, the Mother of God, holding the Child Jesus.

Professor Pattarino was a brilliant artist known for his operatic and comedic renditions in terra-cotta. His figures are often elongated and have tortured facial expressions, but this statue is an exception. Mary's features are beautifully serene. Pattarino's use of drapery is artistically distinctive; this beige gown ornamented by burgundy scrolls is unusual.

*"All glorious is the king's daughter
as she enters,
her raiment threaded with gold;
In embroidered apparel she is led to the king."*
Psalms 45:14-15

Semi-precious stones adorn the crown of Pattarino's Our Lady of the Angels.

Our Lady of Guadalupe Chapel Tilma Relic

A 16th-century relic of Saint Juan Diego's tilma (cloak, miraculously stamped with Mary's image) is revered in a chapel on the north ambulatory, where it is suspended on a 17th-century statue of Our Lady of Guadalupe. Archbishop Luis Maria Martinez of Mexico City gave the square, half-inch relic to Archbishop John Cantwell of Los Angeles in 1941. In 2003 the relic toured to twenty cities throughout the United States in honor of Saint Juan Diego's canonization.

Reconciliation Chapel

The Reconciliation Chapel along the north ambulatory is intended for meditation and for the celebration of the Sacrament of Reconciliation, for the forgiveness of sins and harmony with God. This quiet chapel includes three rooms for confession with screen-separated and face-to-face options. They are spaciously designed to accommodate wheelchair access.

The Art Chapel

Also on the north ambulatory, the Art Chapel is designed to house major traveling exhibits of Christian works of art. The first was a display of liturgical vessels, the cathedra and other works of art from the oldest Catholic cathedral in the United States, the Basilica of the Assumption of the Blessed Virgin Mary in Baltimore, built in 1809.

South Ambulatory

Side chapels along the south ambulatory are used for circulating exhibits celebrating special feast days important to various ethnic groups. Images depicted have been Italian Saint Genaro, Cuban Our Lady of Charity of Cobre, Peruvian Lord of the Miracles, the Dominican Republic's Our Lady of High Grace, and Filipino Our Lady of Antipolo and Santo Nino de Cebu, among others.

●

This fragment of Saint Juan Diego's *tilma* is likely the only one in the United States.

The *Retablo*

The gilded black walnut, Spanish Baroque *retablo* (Spanish word for a "shelf") at the end of the south ambulatory was originally installed behind the altar in the chapel of the Congregation of Saint Philip Neri at Ezcaray, Spain, in 1687. Early in the last century the dismantled retablo was purchased for the Archdiocese of Los Angeles. It was recently restored by Griswold & Associates with financial and technical assistance from the J. Paul Getty Trust. It is 26' wide, 20' high.

"The Spanish *retablo* represents a skill of workmanship, a beauty of design, and a lavishness of ornamentation that have passed from the modern scene," remarks historian Monsignor Francis J. Weber.

43

MUSIC AND LITURGY

"Sing to the Lord a New Song"

From primitive and ancient times, people have always sung to invoke the gods. King David's *Psalms* date from 500 B.C.E. The Catholic Church developed Western music for many centuries, evolving from plainchant to complex choral polyphony. The Cathedral's music ministry aims to continue these long traditions and the multiple cultural traditions of the archdiocese.

Liturgical music enhances worship by giving voice to the beauty of the liturgy's sung prayer. The voices of the Cathedral Choir and of the assembly exist in a dynamic relationship, prefiguring the gathering of the saints and angelic choirs in the New Jerusalem.

The Cathedral Organ

Dobson Pipe Organ Builders, Ltd., of Lake City, Iowa, were commissioned to build the massive Cathedral organ. Rising 85 feet from the floor, it has

Organ Facts:
Biggest pipe: 24" square, made of wood
Front pipes: made of 83% burnished tin
Weight: 42 tons
Wall support: steel structure
Blowers: three, 27-horsepower
Wind pressure range: 5" to 20" water column
Encasement: cherry wood

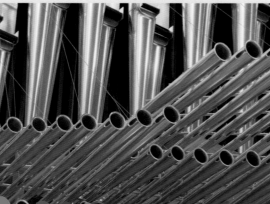

Samuel "Sal" Soria,
Cathedral Organist,
is at the keyboard as
the organ is dedicated
on June 14, 2003.

105 stops and 6019 pipes, including vintage pipes from St. Vibiana Cathedral. It utilizes slider chests with electric pull downs for all manual divisions except the solo and pedal, which have electro-pneumatic action. It is controlled from a moveable console that has four keyboards, or "manuals." A computerized system connects the keys to the valves under each pipe.

The organ's vibrations enable the assembly to feel the music's emotional and physical power.

Cathedral Concerts and Recitals

Through the ages, the Church has made the beauty of music available free to all, royal and peasant alike in the liturgy, as well as in concerts and recitals. The Cathedral continues this tradition with regular musical events, including performances by the Los Angeles Philharmonic, the Los Angeles Master Chorale and church and school choirs.

Acoustical panels are concealed behind the tapestries, above the wood ceiling and high on the back of the transepts' girders. The wood designs on the transept walls provide acoustical diffusion. Engineers used a computer model tested with computer-generated ray diagrams and auralization for both the spoken word and music to identify places needing acoustical treatment.

"**Sing** to the LORD a new song;
sing to the LORD, all the earth." - Psalm 96:1

The Cathedral Choir leads
the congregation
in song on Easter Sunday,
2003, directed by the
Cathedral's Director of
Music Frank Brownstead.

The Master Chorale was one
of the first guest groups
to perform in the Cathedral,
demonstrating its excellent
acoustics, in November, 2002.

45

St. VIBIANA CHAPEL AND SHRINE

Patroness of the Archdiocese

In 1853, in a catacomb near the Appian Way, a tomb was discovered containing the skeleton of a young woman, conjectured by archeologists to have been put to death violently in the 3rd century. An inscription identified her as Vibiana. A year later, Pope Pius IX entrusted the relics to Bishop Thaddeus Amat of Monterey, California, stipulating that his planned cathedral be titled in honor of this Christian martyr.

Saint Vibiana's relics, encased in a reliquary with a golden crown, first resided in the Church of Our Lady of Sorrows in Santa Barbara. In 1868 they were transferred to the Old Plaza Church of *Nuestra Señora de los Angeles* until being moved to the new St. Vibiana Cathedral in 1876. Saint Vibiana was proclaimed the principal patron of the Archdiocese of Los Angeles in 1956.

*A bas relief of **Saint Teresa of Avila**, Patron of Spain, was donated on the occasion of the dedication of the Cathedral by Spanish design architect Professor José Rafael Moneo in honor of his mother. Its inscription recalls the saint's vision of "Our Lady, Queen of the Angels." It hangs over the staircase to the crypt.*

The chapel of Saint Vibiana honors the diocesan patron saint.

St. Vibiana Chapel and Shrine

A chapel on the Cathedral's crypt level is dedicated to Saint Vibiana. Its refashioned marble altar, from St. Vibiana Cathedral, features the Lamb of God, an image of Jesus the innocent victim. The brilliantly painted terra cotta Stations of the Cross were designed by Professor Eugenio Pattarino and came from St. Basil Church in Los Angeles.

In the shrine, a marble sarcophagus contains Saint Vibiana's relics, encased in a wax figure. A replica of the ancient plaque, inscribed "To the soul of the innocent and pure Vibiana," hangs nearby.

This sarcophagus holds the relics of the martyr Saint Vibiana.

Five white marble plaques near Saint Vibiana Chapel and Shrine once surrounded the pulpit at Saint Vibiana Cathedral. They depict Jesus and the four **Evangelists** *(Gospel writers) with their symbols: lion (Mark), man (Matthew), eagle (John), and bull (Luke).*

Saint Mark

Sixth station: Veronica wipes the face of Jesus.

THE CRYPT MAUSOLEUM AND BISHOPS' CRYPT

"I Will Dwell in the House of the Lord Forever"

Like many of the great cathedrals of Europe, the Cathedral of Our Lady of the Angels has a crypt mausoleum on the lower level, near St. Vibiana Chapel. It contains both crypts and cremation niches and is one of very few Cathedral mausoleums in the United States available for the laity. Proceeds from the mausoleum furnish an endowment to assure the Cathedral's financial stability for future generations.

The domed crypt under the main altar faces the Resurrection window.

•

The crypt (from a Greek word meaning "hidden") is the chamber beneath the main level of a church, used for meetings or burials. It developed from the catacombs where the persecuted early Christians worshipped in secret. These were the sites for funerals and held shrines to martyrs and other saints. Early churches often were constructed over the tombs of martyrs. The vaults beneath the main altar developed in the Middle Ages into extensive crypts.

Designed as a prayerful and reflective place, the Cathedral mausoleum is illuminated by alabaster sconces shedding warm light on its Spanish limestone walls. Stained-glass windows and lunettes, lighted from behind, illustrate scenes from the lives of Jesus and Mary.

The Bishops' Crypt

Several cardinals and bishops who served the archdiocese are buried in the Bishops' Crypt within the mausoleum. Fittingly, the exquisite window of Jesus, the Good Shepherd, has a special place here.

● **Jesus is the Good Shepherd (John 10) who carries home the lost lamb. He looks lovingly at the lamb he has rescued, and we are reminded that all people are his lambs.**

The Mausoleum Dome

The dome above the altar crypt, originally from Calvary Cemetery Mausoleum, depicts angels, the Papal tiara (ceremonial hat), Papal awards and the Jerusalem Cross, similar to the one in marble on the sarcophagus. The Latin words translate to:
"At the name of Jesus
every knee should bend,
of those in heaven and on earth and under the earth." - Ph 2:10

Interred or memorialized in the Bishops' Crypt are:
Bishop Francisco Garcia Diego y Moreno,
O.F.M., 1840-46
Bishop Joseph Sadoc Alemany, O.P., 1850-53
Bishop Thaddeus Amat, C.M., 1854-78
Bishop Francis Mora, 1878-96
Bishop George T. Montgomery, 1896-1903
Bishop Thomas Conaty, 1903-1915
Archbishop John J. Cantwell, 1917-47
Cardinal James Francis McIntyre, 1948-70
Cardinal Timothy Manning, 1970-85
Auxiliary Bishop Carl Anthony Fisher, 1987-1993

THE STAINED-GLASS WINDOWS

Artistic Treasures of the Faith

Stained-glass window design and fabrication have not varied much from their medieval origins. The 12th and 13th centuries are considered the Golden Age of stained glass. When most people could not read, stained-glass windows aimed to teach and inspire the faithful by depicting biblical scenes.

Jesus and the Children: "Let the children come to me, and do not prevent them; for the kingdom of heaven belongs to such as these" (Matthew 19:14). A little girl picks daisies, symbolic of innocence, and lily of the valley, an emblem of Jesus suggested by the Song of Songs. She looks like a German country lass, possibly modeled on a child of the artist.

The Commission of Peter: Saint Peter receives from Jesus the authority symbolized by "the keys to the kingdom of heaven. Whatever you bind on earth shall be bound in heaven; and whatever you loose on earth shall be loosed in heaven" (Matthew 16:19). Peter wears blue, the color of heavenly strength, and yellow, the color of truth, like sunlight. He has proclaimed that Jesus is the Messiah, and Jesus gives him responsibility for the church.

St. Cecilia: The patron saint of music is depicted playing a tiny organ. Her clothing combines symbolic colors: white (virginity), red (martyrdom) and blue (strength). Saint Cecilia's hair is a simple series of lines because originally the window was seen at a far distance above the organ in St. Vibiana Cathedral. Cherubs surround her.

Light, line and color remain the essential elements of stained-glass windows. Leaded lines define the areas of color and design. Light awakens the colors, which are the result of metals and metallic oxides painted on and then fired into the glass of these German-style windows. For example, gold is added for ruby color, cobalt for deep blue, and manganese for amethyst, thus comprising the components of some of the precious jewel colors.

The Franz Mayer Company of Munich, Germany, made the mausoleum's sixteen large windows and nine lunettes at the turn of the last century, in Baroque Revival style. They are museum-quality examples of the most beautiful glass of the 19th century. Originally a part of St. Vibiana Cathedral, they were restored by The Judson Studios for installation here.

The Annunciation: Mary, dressed in idealized silk brocade, receives the Angel Gabriel's announcement that she is to be the mother of the Savior. White symbolizes purity; blue is the color of heavenly strength. Mary is depicted reading the Psalms

The Nativity: The infant Jesus radiates light to all around him, as the shepherds join Mary and Joseph in awe

Each window is a splendid example of religious art, rich in symbolic colors and metaphorical images. Each provides inspiration for prayer and meditation on the Scriptures, portraying scenes such as the Annunciation, the Nativity, the Presentation in the Temple, the young Jesus in the Temple, the Garden of Gethsemane, the Resurrection and the Ascension.

The Garden of Gethsemane: Before his Crucifixion, Jesus is in agony on the Mount of Olives. He prays, "Not my will but thine be done."

The Presentation in the Temple: Forty days after the birth of Jesus, Mary complies with the Mosaic Law by going to the Temple to be cleansed and to redeem her first-born, introducing Him into the House of God. Simeon rejoices that he has lived to see the salvation of Israel, and Anna the prophetess recognizes the Savior.

The Resurrection: At sunrise of Easter day, Christ rids the sky of darkness as he rises from his tomb. His triumphal banner is a red cross on a white shield.

The Ascension:
The faces of only ten
apostles are seen as
Jesus rises to heaven.
Judas had hanged
himself. The halo of
the eleventh apostle
is seen at the left of
Jesus' knee. Did the
artist forget the eleventh
apostle? Jesus'garment
blows in the wind, but
neither up nor down,
because the Ascension
prefigures also
the Second Coming.
Jesus is leaving,
but he will return.

53

THE PLAZA AND GARDENS

An Inviting Oasis

The plaza and gardens of the Cathedral are designed to welcome daily visitors. They provide an inviting setting not only for a multitude of liturgical uses, but also for civic and cultural events, fiestas, informal gatherings, noontime lunches, solitary prayer and contemplation.

From the parking garage or the Shepherd's Gate on Temple Street, visitors enter the lower plaza. The Shepherd's Gate, or sheep gate, is a reference to Jesus Christ, the Good Shepherd, who welcomes all. A grand staircase leads to the upper plaza.

The 2.6-acre plaza can hold 5000 people for special celebrations. The crushed granite paving recalls the central plazas of early California mission communities. On the northwest portion are two notable works of art, the Native American Memorial and the Shrine to Our Lady of Guadalupe.

The Cathedral Gift Shop welcomes browsing and the purchase of devotional and commemorative items. The Galero Grill opens onto a tree-shaded patio with tables and colorful chairs.

•
Gift Shop Director Isabel Loriente assists a Cathedral visitor.

54

The Gardens

Each tree and plant species in the plaza and around the Cathedral grounds was chosen for one of several reasons: their Scriptural meanings; Catholic garden traditions, especially as represented in the Franciscan Missions of California; their significance in the liturgical calendar; and the diverse cultural communities of the archdiocese. Thus, for example, the twelve King Palm trees, emblematic of Christ's triumphant entry into Jerusalem on Palm Sunday, lead us to the Cathedral's bronze doors.

The Children's Garden is a grove of olive trees, whose branches have traditionally been symbols of peace. It is designed as a "Discovery" garden where children can find animals sculptures. The whimsical creatures also have symbolic meanings: a dog (faith, loyalty and fidelity), a monkey staring into a

Plaza Trees

King Palms: *The majestic palms represent victory, supremacy, fame, longevity, resurrection and immortality.*

Japanese Maples: *Traditional in Japanese gardens, they are the most delicate of all maples.*

Valencia Oranges: *Planted for ornamental and shade purposes in mission gardens, they yield delicious fruit.*

Mission Figs: *One of the characteristic trees in mission gardens, used by Jesus in his parables.*

Chinese Flame Trees: *Planted in Chinese courtyard gardens for centuries, they are known for a fall display of salmon-colored seedpods.*

True Green Evergreen Elms: *A Chinese garden tradition, they cast dappled shade.*

Olive trees: *Planted in a quincunx grid, equally spaced in every direction, they are a hallmark of the cultivated California landscape.*

Coast Live Oak and California Valley Oak: *They will grow to about 50 feet, symbols of might, endurance, longevity and nobility.*

California Fan Palms: *The only palm native to California was a favorite of the missions.*

Chilean Wine Palms: *Native to Chile, this species is crowned by feather fronds.*

Fairmont Ginkgoes: *Native to Asia, they are grown adjacent to temples in China as a symbol of immortality and in Japan as an emblem of loyalty.*

Italian Stone Pine: *This classic, umbrella shaped pine of Rome is a rich chestnut brown, its needles deep green.*

California Peppers: *Reminiscent of trees planted at the mission stable yards, these trees line the base of the parking garage's freeway edge.*

The **Donor Wall** on the north side of the plaza commemorates the Cathedral's major benefactors, the "angels" who made the building of the Cathedral complex possible. Sixteen angels form a continuous band, designed and hand-etched on laminated glass by Russian-trained Armenian artist Hakob Jambazian of The Judson Studios of Los Angeles. In front of the angels, who seem to float over the Hollywood Freeway, are glass panels with donors' names etched in the glass.

mirrored reflection ball (spontaneity) and a lion (God's might), among others. A donkey is inscribed with the words, "Better a donkey you have to encourage than one that won't carry its load." Inside the whale is an inscription "Jonah was here."

Mission gardens have a long tradition in California. When Fray Junipero Serra founded the first California mission in San Diego in 1769, he and his followers brought contributions to horticulture from Southern Europe and the Mediterranean. Serra planted the seeds of the date palm as early as 1770. The Franciscans also brought to the twenty-one missions wine grapes and varieties of trees, such as olive, eucalyptus, pomegranate, fig, lemon, orange, apple, pear and peach.

●
These lambs in the Children's Garden are learning to walk.

Well-known architects Douglas and Regula Campbell of Campbell & Campbell in Santa Monica, California, designed the Cathedral's gardens and landscaping with plants capable of thriving in the urban environment with relatively low resource and maintenance requirements.

●
Queen Palms (left) and Zeheti Palms (right) frame the campanile.

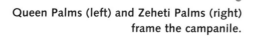

$\mathcal{T}$HE FOUNTAINS

"I Shall Give You Living Water"

T he Cathedral plaza features three fountains with flowing water, evoking thoughts of the living waters of Baptism. The Gateway Pool and Water Wall, the Jerusalem Fountain and the Meditation Garden Fountain all provide a soothing, cooling respite from the bustle of the nearby Civic Center.

*"**Streams** of the river gladden the city of God, the holy dwelling of the Most High." - Psalm 46:5*

The Cathedral continues the tradition of the Franciscans, who brought their Spanish-influenced central fountains to the courtyards of the California Missions in the 1700s. Each fountain has a special significance.

The Gateway Pool and Water Wall

Near the Shepherd's Gate off Temple Street is the disc-shaped Gateway Pool designed by California artist Lita Albuquerque. In the pool are words sandblasted out of the marble: "I shall give you living water," rendered in 36 languages currently spoken at Masses in the 290 parish churches in the Archdiocese of Los Angeles. Jesus spoke these words to the Samaritan woman he met at the well (John 4:4-26). He reached out to her across the separations of race and gender, asking this outcast for water and promising her "living water."

Water flows constantly from the Water Wall and is a precursor of the flowing water that washes away sin, to be seen in the baptistery inside the Cathedral.

Water gushes up within the Gateway Pool. The Water Wall is on the right.

The Jerusalem Fountain

*"They shall not hunger or **thirst**." - Isaiah 49:10*

On the north side of the plaza, adjacent to the Children's Garden, is the Jerusalem Fountain, donated by the Jewish community through the Skirball Foundation to celebrate the ties between Judaism and Catholicism. It is inscribed with the words of Shimon the Righteous, "Three pillars uphold the world: divine teaching, ethical service, and loving kindness." He taught that for the sake of these three activities God created the world.

A contemporary of Alexander the Great, Shimon was a High Priest of the ancient Jewish Temple. His title "the righteous" honored his piety and kindness. His words portray an ideal to strive for: to be close to God and of benefit to humanity.

The rose and golden limestones in the Jerusalem Fountain come from an ancient quarry outside the walled city of Jerusalem.

The Meditation Garden Fountain

Near the campanile, outside the north ambulatory, a quiet pool in the Meditation Garden invites contemplation. The life-giving water flows over a giant boulder into waters filled with lilies. The pool and garden, surrounded by Queen and Zehiti palms, Japanese maples and sycamores, are conducive to quiet reflection.

"In green pastures you let me graze;
*to safe **waters** you lead me;*
you restore my strength." - Psalm 23:2,3

The boulders in the Meditation Garden were collected from among the hills within the archdiocese.

"Ring in the Christ That Is to Be"

The Carillon

Is there a person who does not pause to hear the pealing of church bells as they ring the hours of our days? Surely, the ill and infirm in nearby hospitals and rest homes hear the sound of solace, the prisoners in city jails and the homeless hear the sound of hope, and the lonely and elderly hear the sound of God's love.

Above the Shepherd's Gate threshold bordering Temple Street is the carillon wall. It contains 37 stationary bells programmed to ring the hours and to call people to worship.

Thirty-five of these bells, manufactured in the late 1920s in Belgium, originally hung at St. Monica Church, Santa Monica. When the 1971 earthquake damaged that bell tower, they were installed at the San Fernando Mission until being moved here. The half-ton bourdon-bell was engineered to strike the hours, while a second large bell counted off the half hours.

*"For **bells** are the voice of the church; they have tones that touch and search the hearts of young and old." - Longfellow*

*"The sounding of church bells **rings** out a clarion message of good news: we are redeemed, even we sinners, and summoned by the bells to a close intimacy with God." - Cardinal Roger Mahony, Dedication homily*

THE BELLS

The largest bell in the carillon comes from St. Timothy Church in Los Angeles. It was originally one of 48 bells manufactured in Belgium in 1929 for William Randolph Hearst's San Simeon.

This bell from St. Timothy Church is the largest in the Shepherd Gate carillon. It is inscribed "Ring out the darkness of the land, Ring in the Christ that is to be," and "Ring in the valiant man and free the larger heart, the kindlier hand."

The carillon over the Shepherd Gate recalls the significance of bells in early California mission life.

The Campanile

The campanile (Italian for "bell tower") at the northwest corner of the Cathedral complex rises 156 feet and is topped by a 25-foot cross. It is built of the same architectural concrete as the Cathedral. Following tradition from the Middle Ages, it is free-standing.

The campanile is built to hold 18 swinging bells; four are now in place: two from St. Vibiana Cathedral, cast in the 1880s, and two from churches in the archdiocese.

The tower is a piece of sculpture that relies on subtle transformations. Slight shifts in its planes reflect different lights, giving it vibrancy as the sun plays with it from morning to night.

The **campanile** sits on four friction pendulum bearings which resemble stainless steel saucers, shallow bowls six feet in diameter with a stainless steel puck about sixteen inches in diameter. The lateral force is absorbed in an 8.5 earthquake by the pucks sliding up to 30 inches in the bowl to prevent the tall structure from falling. This is the first use in downtown Los Angeles of this design, originally engineered for bridges.

Four bells are mounted in the campanile.

The Patroness of the Americas

Shrine to Our Lady of Guadalupe

O ur Lady of Guadalupe, the patroness of the Americas, is a traditional and powerful symbol for Mexicans and Mexican-Americans. Designed by Mexican-born artist Lalo Garcia, the shrine on the north plaza wall represents the appearance of Mary, Jesus' mother, to Saint Juan Diego near Mexico City in 1531.

Saint Juan Diego, whom Mary called "my dearest and youngest son."

A skeptical Bishop Juan de Zumarraga first rejected Mary's request to Juan that a church be built in her name. Mary again appeared and guided Juan, speaking to him in his native Aztec *Nahuatl*. At her instruction he collected roses in the cold of December. Later, in front of the bishop, he opened his *tilma* (cape) and revealed the roses. Much to the surprise of both Juan and the bishop, Mary's image was imprinted on his simple robe.

*T*HE SHRINES

The shrine has two mosaic-style images, a twelve-foot replica facing the Hollywood Freeway and a triptych facing the plaza. Garcia chose *talavera* (Mexican tile). "I wanted to make the tile from Mexican soil, Mexican clay, labored over by Mexican hands," he says.

The image of Our Lady of Guadalupe overlooks the Hollywood Freeway.

On the left panel of the plaza triptych is Saint Juan Diego. In the center is a stylized *tilma* with a digital representation of Our Lady of Guadalupe, photographed from the original in Mexico City. She appeared as a young, pregnant, Spanish-Aztec woman, wearing an Aztec maternity sash. Mary's cape is held by two angels, one Aztec, one Spanish, to remind us of the encounter of the Native American and the European and the resulting *mestizo* in Mexico.

An Aztec angel holds the left corner of Mary's cape.

The third panel is a collage of children's faces, representing multi-ethnic Angelinos and all the children of the world.

Native American Memorial

The theme of pilgrimage, of the journey of faith, inspired sculptor Johnny Bear Contreras as he created the 4.8' bronze Native American Memorial for the northwest plaza. The lower portion of the 600-pound sculpture captures the ocean tide flowing to the sand and onto the reefs. It reflects many Native American songs and ceremonies referring to earth's natural rhythms. Contreras is a member of the Kumeyaay tribe of San Diego, California.

"Man can be moving like liquid," says Johnny Bear **Contreras**, *"or sedentary like stone."*

A human figure symbolizes the emergence of humanity from within the natural world as part of the creation story. Its left arm grasps the reef, either to propel forward or to find stability. The sculpture thus deals with life's dual energies and with human beings in transition. Rock steps represent the journey and struggle for higher planes of understanding.

"Non fecit taliter omni nationi" (*"God has not done this for other nations"* - Psalm 147:20) declared Pope Benedict XIV in 1751 when Father Juan Lopez gave him an image of Our Lady of Guadalupe painted by Miguel Goatherd. These words appear on the triptych's right panel.

"Love one another as I have loved you"

The Cathedral of Our Lady of the Angels is firmly planted in downtown Los Angeles, a city filled with people who work in high-rise buildings and return home to suburbs for dinner. Left behind are the estimated 5000 working poor, newly arrived immigrants and the homeless who inhabit the nearby hillsides below Dodger Stadium and the streets of skid row. As a parish, the Cathedral ministers to the local community.

Cathedral volunteers donate countless hours preparing sandwiches and working with Jóvenes, Inc., an outreach organization, to provide food to the homeless sleeping under bridges and to day laborers standing on corners waiting to be hired.

Cathedral volunteers visit the prisoners at Central Juvenile Hall and Men's Central Jail, offering listening ears and words of compassion. They lead daily informational and inspirational tours at the Cathedral, assisting visitors to experience their journey with depth and understanding.

Cathedral Charities is in its infancy. What began as help to the poor and disenfranchised with the Cathedral's Outreach Center is expanding to assist neighboring parishes and community centers. Mobile medical and eye clinics and housing assistance address critical needs. The mission of the Cathedral is to welcome all brothers and sisters and to minister to them in the spirit of Jesus Christ, to serve them directly or to make referrals to existing services.

The Outreach Center's vision is to reach out in new directions to society's vulnerable people. Achieving goals depends upon God's guidance, the generosity of donors and the hard work of volunteers.

> "Be kind to one another, **compassionate**."
> - Ephesians 4:32
>
> •
>
> "For this reason I kneel before the Father... that Christ may dwell in your hearts through faith; that you, rooted and grounded in love, may have strength to comprehend with all the holy ones what is the breadth and length and height and depth, and to know the **love** of Christ that surpasses knowledge, so that you may be filled with all the fullness of God."
> - Ephesians 3:14, 17-19

Volunteer Gerald Fagan
guides Cathedral visitors,
enhancing
their understanding
and spiritual encounter.

*A*CKNOWLEDGMENTS

•

Editor
Mary-Cabrini Durkin

•

Photography
Cathedral photographs by
  Frantisek Zvardon
Dedication photographs
  Photos by Lee Salem Photography,
  Inc.: pages 10, 13b, 19, 33a, 38
  Photograph by Armando Arorizo:
  page 45a
  Photographs by Terry Casaus:
  pages 37a, 45c
  Photograph by Karina Pires: page
  45b
Courtesy of Cathedral of Our Lady of
the Angels Archives, Archdiocese of
Los Angeles:
  Tom Wilmshurst Photography:
  pages 8c, 9b
  Warren Aerial Photography, Inc.:
  pages 5, 16
Photograph by Douglas Jungwirth:
page 54b
Historic photos, Courtesy of
Archdiocese of Los Angeles: pages
7b, c, d; 8a; 9a

•

Excerpts from
the *New American Bible with Revised
New Testament and Psalms*
Copyright (c) 1991, 1986, 1970
Confraternity of Christian Doctrine,
Inc., Washington, DC. Used with
permission. All rights reserved.
No part of the *New American Bible*
may be reproduced by any means
without permission in writing from
the copyright owner.

•

Published by
Éditions du Signe
BP 94 – 67038 Strasbourg
Cedex 2 – France
Tel (++33) 3 88 78 91 91
Fax (++33) 3 88 78 91 99
info@editionsdusigne.fr

•

Publishing Director
Christian Riehl

•

Director of Publication
Joëlle Bernhard

•

Publishing Assistant
Audrey Gilger

•

Layout
Sylvie Tusinski

•

Photoengraving
Éditions du Signe-105933

© Éditions du Signe 2005
ISBN 2-7468-1400-5
All rights reserved - Reproduction
forbidden

Printed in China by Sun Fung Offset
Binding, Co., Ltd.